CW00546212

Boutros Boutros-Ghali

New Dimensions of
Arms Regulation and Disarmament
in the Post–Cold War Era

Report of the Secretary-General

United Nations

Department of Political Affairs

A/C.1/47/7

PREFACE

On 27 October 1992, during the observance of Disarmament Week, the Secretary-General of the United Nations issued a report entitled "New Dimensions of Arms Regulation and Disarmament in the Post–Cold War Era".* The changed international environment has created new opportunities for the pursuit of disarmament, as well as posing new challenges.

In introducing his report, the Secretary-General noted that the end of bipolarity has not diminished the need for disarmament; if anything, it has increased it. He emphasized that disarmament is an inherent part of preventive diplomacy, peacemaking, peace-keeping and peace-building, four areas for action by the international community that he examined in his earlier report "An Agenda for Peace".**

The present publication reproduces the Secretary-General's report and includes, in annexes, illustrative information relevant to disarmament and arms control efforts.

* A/C.1/47/7.

**A/47/277-S/24111 of 17 June 1992. The report was issued as a United Nations publication (DPI/1247).

Contents

Report of the Secretary-General of the United Nations

INTRODUCTION

1. Few aspects of international life have changed more profoundly in recent years than the pursuit of arms regulation and disarmament. A decade ago, negotiations in this field were characterized by tension and acrimony. All of us recall that time of widespread public apprehension over the alarming escalation in the arms race, the nuclear arms race in particular, and the disquieting rise in military expenditures world wide. Today, the situation is dramatically different. Significant progress has been achieved in a number of important areas of disarmament. The whole international political structure is in a process of transformation. The world has become a little safer, but considerably more complicated. The changed international environment has created new opportunities for the pursuit of disarmament, as well as posing new challenges. It is evident that many of the tasks and methods used by the international community in the past should be reviewed and reformed.

2. In the recent past it was normal to treat disarmament as if it were little more than a utopian vision, safely confined to a distant future. Now that real arms reductions are occurring it has become usual in some quarters to view disarmament as a facet of the cold war that is no longer centrally relevant to international security needs. I strongly disagree with this proposition.

3. The observance of Disarmament Week gives me the opportunity to address the complex issues of disarmament and international security. I will concentrate on those which in my view are of primary importance.

4.   First, it is my strong feeling that the time has come for the practical integration of disarmament and arms regulation issues into the broader structure of the international peace and security agenda. Traditionally, disarmament has been perceived as a relatively distinct subject which required its own separate organizational framework. We now need to realize that disarmament constitutes an integral part of international efforts to strengthen international peace and security. Problems in this field can be resolved only in conjunction with other political and economic issues, while solutions to political and economic issues are often found in conjunction with disarmament measures.

5.   Secondly, a globalization of the process of arms control and disarmament is now needed. It is vital that all States be engaged in the process of disarmament and that they give practical content to their declared intent. Globalization of the process of disarmament implies an all-inclusive, multidimensional, non-compartmentalized approach.

6.   And thirdly, we need to build upon, and revitalize, past achievements in arms regulation and reduction. There have been impressive accomplishments in reducing strategic and nuclear weapons. Important advances towards peace have been made in Latin America, Africa and Asia. In the world's most heavily armed region—Europe—the process of conventional disarmament is gathering momentum. The Treaty on the Non-Proliferation of Nuclear Weapons now enjoys the adherence of 154 States. The comprehensive prohibition on chemical weapons is at long last becoming a reality. These

significant trends must be further encouraged and developed.

7. These three concepts—integration, globalization and revitalization—can be the foundation-stones of an enhanced international effort in the field of disarmament and arms regulation. Conceptually, none of them is fundamentally novel. Many scholars and theorists have written about them for years. What is new is that these goals are now achievable, provided we take concerted and well-focused actions.

I. INTEGRATION. DISARMAMENT IN THE NEW INTERNATIONAL ENVIRONMENT

8.   In recent years, much time and energy have been spent on developing the rules and techniques of negotiation.   As a result it is sometimes hard to keep sight of broader objectives, and in particular, of the links which exist between disarmament and arms regulation on the one hand, and the political processes that shape international behaviour on the other. These connections, however, are crucial to progress both in the field of disarmament and in the creation of a new system of international security.

9.   Although we have taken some strides in dealing with excesses in armaments and military expenditures, the world remains a dangerous place: the shadows of the weaponry of mass destruction still loom large; the threat of weapons proliferation—be it nuclear, chemical, biological or conventional—still exists; the trade in weapons is again gaining momentum; and military expenditures in many parts of the world are still far too excessive in relation to unmet human needs.

10.   Today there is a real opportunity to initiate a process of global disarmament. This should be closely coordinated with efforts in other fields and should be seen as part of the larger network of international cooperative behaviour which is designed to safeguard the security of all nations. Disarmament, the structuring of a new system of international relations and improving economic conditions should be regarded as complementary measures and as far as possible should be implemented in a coordinated manner. This can be seen more

clearly when we consider current United Nations efforts to resolve regional conflicts.

11. In my report, "An Agenda for Peace" (A/47/277-S/24111), I address the changing nature of the world Organization's work in three specific areas of conflict resolution—preventive diplomacy, peacemaking and peace-keeping—as well as in the added challenges incumbent in post-conflict "peace-building". Each of these areas has its own requirements. All of them can be supported and strengthened by concrete measures of arms regulation and disarmament. There is, in short, a constructive parallel between conflict resolution and disarmament: the two go hand in hand. Our effectiveness in addressing the maintenance of international peace and security through these tools of preventive diplomacy, peacemaking, peace-keeping and peace-building will determine the extent to which the international community will make progress in achieving concrete disarmament measures, thus allowing for significant reductions in weapons arsenals and military expenditures.

12. In particular, in the context of peace-keeping and peace-building operations, the role for arms limitation can be significant. In places such as the Golan Heights, El Salvador, Cambodia and Angola, to name but a few, United Nations peace-keepers have become well versed in the mechanics of conducting weapons inspections and monitoring troop withdrawals or disengagement zones. Current trends indicate that these kinds of activities will expand in the future. The integration of weapons-control features into United Nations-brokered settlements can contribute enormously to peace-building activities in countries long plagued by civil strife. What could be closer

7

to the true spirit of disarmament than to demobilize tens of thousands of soldiers, to dispose of their arms and to develop new techniques for removing millions of land-mines that threaten innocent civilians in former combat zones?

13.   There is another domain of conflict resolution where the use of disarmament measures may be required: peace enforcement. Disarmament and inspection procedures are playing a concrete role in the implementation of Security Council resolution 687 (1991) of 3 April 1991 concerning Iraq. United Nations personnel have been directly involved in achieving important milestones regarding the implementation of disarmament measures. The use of disarmament measures within the framework of peace enforcement is quite distinct from the process of disarmament through negotiation, which several States and elements of the international community have been pursuing for years. The two should never be confused, even if there may be some conceptual overlap in terms of the mechanics of weapons inspection and disposal. I fervently hope that the global community will not have to face again the circumstances of war as recently experienced in the Persian Gulf region. But let us resolve that, in the face of grave violations of disarmament agreements or of other threats to peace, this Organization will be ready to act in accordance with its responsibilities under its Charter.

II. GLOBALIZATION. ENHANCING THE MULTILATERAL APPROACH

14.   What has happened in the relationship between the two major military Powers, the Russian Federation and the United States of America, is remarkable. A period of confrontation, hostility and mistrust has been replaced by a spirit of cooperation that has enabled them to attain far-reaching disarmament agreements and increased mutual trust. This has permitted each to undertake unilaterally profound nuclear disarmament measures—notably in the field of tactical nuclear weapons—which augurs well for the institution of confidence-building as an important element of the evolving international security system. Such steps should not be confined to the exclusive domain of these two nations. We must strive to create conditions in other regions of the world which would enable more States to undertake similar commitments. This is what some call disarmament by mutual example or reciprocated unilateral measures. Such measures, while most helpful and desirable, are a first important step in the globalization of the disarmament process.

15.   The goal is to extend disarmament efforts to include not only bilateral agreements but also multilateral arrangements in a world-wide process involving all States. The argument advanced by some States that the major military Powers should disarm first is too often used to avoid practical disarmament measures and is no longer valid. It is possible today for the reduction and regulation of armaments to take place without putting national security at risk. Such measures could be

implemented on different levels—global, regional and subregional.

16.   I am encouraged to see growing interest among many States in developing regional approaches to arms limitation and confidence-building. This trend is to be encouraged. Fundamentally, it is up to States to decide for themselves what kind of arms regulations appear to be the most sensible in the light of local conditions. The types of proposals adopted in one region or subregion may not be applicable to another. At the same time, one can imagine numerous ways in which regional approaches could enhance the process of global arms reduction. Regional and subregional organizations can further the globalization of disarmament, both in cooperation with each other and with the United Nations.

17.   On the regional level, for example, there is an evident need to devote major attention to the question of conventional arms races. For years, concern was concentrated, and rightly so, on the need to halt the nuclear arms race and to achieve concrete measures of nuclear disarmament. As a result, too little was done to address the highly destabilizing effect on regional and subregional security resulting from the transfers of conventional weapons which went far beyond the legitimate security needs of States. The relentless accumulation of armaments by States is not only a symptom of political tension; it can also cause and heighten such tensions and increase the risk of conflict. The detrimental effect of these weapons transfers on regional security and stability continues to be felt today, particularly in connection with the continuing transfer of weapons to volatile areas such

as the Middle East, which has been the recipient of over 30 per cent of world weapons imports.

18. I am confident that international organizations can do a better job in serving as a focus for serious discussions of an interregional nature. International organizations in general and those of the United Nations system in particular can play a much more significant role in the globalization of disarmament.

III. REVITALIZATION. BUILDING ON PAST ACHIEVEMENTS

19.   To achieve genuine disarmament we have to complete the building of a new system of international security. This new system must cope with the new dimensions of insecurity as well as the complexities of achieving international peace. To be viable, it has to instil sufficient confidence in States to assure them that they no longer need abundant weaponry. This would lead to considerable reductions in their arsenals and corresponding reductions in military expenditures.

20.   The cold war did not carry the cause of disarmament and arms limitation far enough, but it left an important legacy in the form of a system of agreements and treaties. These provide a solid framework for furthering the disarmament and arms control process today. There are in existence some 11 global multilateral agreements, 4 major regional multilateral agreements, and 16 bilateral agreements concluded solely by the United States and the Russian Federation. These are not negligible numbers—all the more so when we consider that they cover a wide range of issues from weapons of mass destruction and conventional weapons, to confidence-building measures. This is a solid foundation to build upon now that the conditions for progress in this field have been enhanced.

A. Weapons of mass destruction

21.   Traditionally, this category of capability has been of paramount concern, and remains so today. Over the years, the thrust of diplomacy has been to reduce and,

wherever possible, to eliminate these weapons; to curb their proliferation among States; and to preclude their deployment in certain international domains, such as outer space, the seabed and Antarctica.

22.   At long last, we are on the verge of historic accomplishments. The process of nuclear disarmament is gathering momentum, at least as it relates to the United States and the States of the former Soviet Union. By the end of this decade, the multiple-warhead intercontinental ballistic missile (ICBM) may be a thing of the past, and the category of tactical nuclear weapons will be sharply reduced, if not totally eliminated. The scope of nuclear-weapon limitations agreed to by these two major nations is absolutely striking, as is evident from simple statistics. The 1991 START Treaty* will reduce the total number of long-range nuclear warheads in the United States arsenals to some 8,550, compared with 12,640 in 1990. The Russian Federation will retain some 6,160 warheads, compared with the 11,000 held by the former Soviet Union in 1990. The agreement reached last June between the two sides, when translated into treaty language, could by the end of this century leave the United States with as few as 3,500 and the Russian Federation with as few as 3,000 warheads. This would represent a reduction of approximately 70 per cent over the next decade.

23.   Now that reductions are occurring, a number of questions assume greater importance: How could

*Treaty between the United States of America and the Union of Soviet Socialist Republics on the Reduction and Limitation of Strategic Offensive Arms, signed on 31 July 1991.

envisioned cuts lead to even further reductions? When will the negotiating process be enlarged to include other nuclear-weapon States? And will the parties, having already sharply curtailed their qualitative improvement programmes, finally agree to halt nuclear testing completely?

24.   The international community can aim for no less a goal than the complete elimination of nuclear weapons. Achieving this goal may take some time. Nuclear technology cannot be disinvented; and there are a host of difficult questions—including issues of stability and verification—which must be weighed carefully. It is my belief, nevertheless, that the full array of hazards posed to humanity by these weapons cannot be adequately dealt with until we have crossed the threshold of the post-nuclear-weapon age.

25.   In this context, a comprehensive ban on nuclear testing would be a significant step leading to the goal of the elimination of all nuclear weapons. The seriousness of purpose demonstrated by the two major Powers as they continue to reduce their nuclear arsenals drastically, and the ongoing efforts by the international community to prevent the proliferation of nuclear weapons, can best be matched by embracing the associated measure of halting the qualitative improvement of nuclear weapons through a cessation of nuclear testing. The annual number of tests carried out in the last several years indicates a most welcome downward trend. In only two years, from 1987 to 1989, the number of tests dropped from 47 to 27. This was followed by further reductions to 18 tests in 1990 and 14 in 1992. I strongly welcome the current moratoria put into effect by some nuclear-weapon

States. Gradual and significant reductions in the number and yield of tests are options which should be encouraged in a progressive move towards a total ban on nuclear testing.

26. Fortunately, with respect to chemical arms, the international community is on the verge of just such an achievement. We have before us the long-awaited draft Convention on a Comprehensive Prohibition of Chemical Weapons which has been completed by the Conference on Disarmament. I am aware of the fact that certain aspects of this Convention are not as every State would like. On the whole, however, I believe that this agreement deserves your support. As there are today some 20 States that possess or seek to acquire a chemical weapons capability, this Convention, along with universal adherence to the Convention banning biological weapons, is an indispensable element in global efforts to deal effectively with weapons of mass destruction.

B. Proliferation control

27. Current international trends should help immeasurably in achieving a priority which is of growing importance to the global community—the non-proliferation of weapons. At a moment when substantial disarmament is finally beginning to occur, there can be no justification for any State, anywhere, to acquire the tools and technologies of mass destruction. This judgement, I believe, is widely shared by States. It was articulated clearly at the Security Council Summit last January, when the Council declared that the proliferation of nuclear, and indeed all weapons of mass destruction, constituted a threat to international peace and security.

The question is how to turn the logic of non-proliferation into concerted action.

28.   In the nuclear realm, the Non-Proliferation Treaty continues to provide an indispensable framework for our global non-proliferation efforts. All of us know all too well that the Treaty has its contentious aspects. And yet the broad adherence, which now includes all the nuclear-weapon States, emphasizes its fundamental validity. It is clear, however, that verification and safeguards arrangements for the Treaty need to be strengthened. When the Treaty itself comes up for extension in 1995, it should be extended indefinitely and unconditionally. *All States should adhere to the Treaty.*

29.   Over the longer term, it is my hope that we may achieve more equitable and comprehensive approaches to responsible proliferation control, not only of weapons but also of long-range delivery systems and dual-use technologies. To be fully effective, such controls must be balanced and fair; they must not unduly hamper the peaceful uses of science and technology; and they should not divide the world into the invidious categories of "haves" and "have-nots".

C. Arms transfers

30.   The problems related to excessive arms transfers are daunting. Paradoxically, this is attributable, in part, to the success achieved in disarmament negotiations. Production overcapacities and surplus equipment in industrialized States are now increasingly feeding arms markets in parts of the developing world. Measured in constant 1988 United States dollars, arms transfers rose

from $14 billion per year in the early 1960s to about $50 billion in 1988.

31.   In this connection I would like to recommend to States to take a closer look at international private "arms dealers". In the present situation it is both possible and necessary to impose stricter regulations on such activities.

32.   Unfortunately, one obstacle that stands in the way of effective global controls is the difficulty of objectively distinguishing between defensive and provocative arms transfers. One potentially valuable alternative would be regional agreements on what constitutes clearly excessive or threatening conventional military capabilities. Ideally, such agreements could help reduce both the supply of, and the demand for, advanced weaponry, but in ways that would not undermine the security of States that rely on arms imports for legitimate defensive needs.

33.   Further, the "opportunity costs" incurred, particularly by developing countries through unduly high military expenditures, serve as grim reminders of the need for restraint in weapons transfers. Education is only one sector that could greatly benefit from the increased availability of resources. While Governments are spending an average of $36,000 per year per member of the armed forces, 30 times more than they invest in the education of each enrolled child, a 1990 World Bank report reveals that an increase of only one year in average years of education may lead to a 3 per cent rise in gross domestic product.

17

D. Transparency in arms and other confidence-building measures

34.   I am encouraged by the steady progress that is being made towards the goal of increased transparency in armaments. To be sure, transparency is no substitute for reductions in arms, but when properly applied, it can be conducive to confidence-building among States and helpful in alerting the global community to excessive accumulations of armaments. Thus, it could serve as another useful tool in facilitating non-proliferation efforts.

35.   In this context, the newly created United Nations Register of Conventional Arms, which was the subject of much debate last year, assumes even greater practical importance. The panel of experts which was assembled to develop technical procedures for the Register and to study the modalities of its future expansion was able to adopt its report by consensus. I commend the results of its work, and I urge Member States to embrace their recommendations so that we may give the Register a strong foundation and the broadest possible participation by States.

36.   For my part, I wish to assure you that this Organization will do all that it can to make the Register an efficient and successful service for Member States. For your part, it is vitally important that sufficient resources be made available for this task. Nothing would undermine the Register's operation more quickly than inadequate attention to the funding which is necessary to make it an effective instrument.

37.   In politics, as in everyday life, problems often arise from misinterpreted intentions. Thus openness and

transparency are crucially important as part of the process of building confidence. Their significance must be emphasized, particularly at regional and subregional levels, in order to make military behaviour more predictable and to reassure concerned States of the non-threatening intentions of potential rivals. Openness and transparency can also be useful early-warning instruments in the process of preventive diplomacy.

IV. CONCLUSION. NEW CHALLENGES

A. Conversion

38.   With the development of the process of disarmament we are encountering an entirely new set of problems, which may be labelled "post-disarmament issues". The correlation between disarmament measures and economic conditions has drawn more attention over recent years as democratic trends influence development. This emerging issue highlights the immediate need for post-disarmament efforts as economies and Governments try to transform military-oriented industrial complexes into enterprises serving social, humanitarian and development needs. Three problems stand out in urgency and complexity: the safe destruction and storage of armaments resulting from disarmament agreements; conversion of military capacities to peaceful uses; and adequate technical and financial facilities to make this transition in a balanced manner.

39.   As we have recently learned, disarmament measures may entail significant transaction expense. The long-term savings are clearly of a much greater magnitude, but finding ways and means to deal with the environmental hazards and the related expenses of dismantling weapons is a major concern. To initiate the conversion from military to civilian production, significant advances in the reduction and limitation of armaments are needed. On the other hand, the existence of huge military production capacities makes disarmament an uncertain development. Conversion, as is apparent from recent experience, is not an easy task; it requires great effort and sacrifice. In many countries, in particular

economically advanced ones, there are large segments of the population dependent on military production. Restructuring industry and retraining skilled and unskilled labour will have a debilitating effect on many economies. The arms industry and the military establishment, which usually enjoy considerable privileges, will resist changes. Unless States take decisive actions in changing this situation, disarmament will be a slower and more painful process.

40. These requirements are substantial, but they are not beyond the bounds of creative diplomacy. The United Nations stands ready to assist in exploring these concepts. It is an appropriate forum to foster dialogue on this matter so that effective, yet non-discriminatory, ways may be found to deal with this matter. Advanced economies must share their expertise and experience with other nations.

41. As disarmament agreements are implemented, an environmentally sound and safe system for the destruction of weapons is of prime importance. Technical assistance and the capacity for the safe transport and long-term storage of highly toxic weapons material have also become a necessary concern.

42. The financial and ecological burdens of effective weapons disposal are the immediate, and unavoidable, consequences of implementing reductions. Much more far-reaching is the problem of redirecting manufacturing and research-and-development capacities, as well as soldiers and technical personnel, from military to civilian endeavours. I urge all States to consider methods to alleviate the problems of making the painful transition to a post-disarmament world. On my part, I am establish-

ing an interdepartmental task force at the United Nations to provide Member States with political, technical and economic advice on the various aspects involved in such a transition.

B. New machinery

43. The United Nations framework in which disarmament has been pursued was created in the course of the cold war. This machinery should be reassessed in order to meet the new realities and priorities of our time. What we need is a coordinated system which would allow the international community to address major disarmament problems promptly, flexibly and efficiently.

44. I support greater Security Council involvement in disarmament matters, and in particular, the enforcement of non-proliferation. In this regard, it should be recalled that under the Charter of the United Nations the Military Staff Committee is to provide assistance to the Security Council on all questions relating, *inter alia*, to the regulation of armaments and possible disarmament.

45. Over the past two years the Conference on Disarmament has engaged in a process of self-examination. The time has come to proceed from exploratory discussions to practical actions. In my opinion, a comprehensive approach is needed to address the structure, functions, methods of work and working agenda of the Conference on Disarmament. The efforts of the Conference on Disarmament might be focused on well-defined and urgent issues. The Conference on Disarmament could also be considered as a permanent review and supervisory body for some existing multilateral arms regulations and disarmament agreements.

46. In today's world, societies can no longer afford to solve problems by the use of force. All the aims and priorities I have discussed are practical and obtainable; none is utopian. In international politics, one of the most important means of reducing violence in inter-State relations is disarmament. What is required of States is concerted efforts and broad participation. Let us hope that as future generations look back on this period, they will say that we were truly able to make arms limitation and disarmament a commonplace part of international life.

Annexes

Special Sessions of the United Nations General Assembly Devoted to Disarmament

Tenth special session of the General Assembly (first special session devoted to disarmament)

Dates: 23 May–30 June 1978

Document issued: Final Document of the Tenth Special Session (A/S-10/4, sect. III), adopted by consensus, stressed that the United Nations had a central role and primary responsibility in the field of disarmament, in accordance with its Charter. The Document included a programme of action, through the implementation of which progress towards general and complete disarmament could be achieved. The programme contained priorities and enumerated specific measures of disarmament.

Twelfth special session of the General Assembly (second special session devoted to disarmament)

Dates: 7 June–10 July 1982

Document issued: Concluding Document of the Twelfth Special Session (A/S-12/32), adopted by consensus, was largely procedural in nature. It reaffirmed the validity of the 1978 Final Document and also launched a World Disarmament Campaign, now known as the United Nations Disarmament Information Programme.

Fifteenth special session of the General Assembly (third special session devoted to disarmament)

Dates: 31 May–25 June 1988

Document issued: Consensus on a substantive concluding document was not achieved.

United Nations Studies and Reports in the Field of Disarmament Carried Out by the Secretary-General (1988–1992)

Study on the Climatic and Other Global Effects of Nuclear War (A/43/351): carried out by the Secretary-General with the assistance of consultant experts pursuant to General Assembly resolutions 40/152 G and 41/86 H and submitted to the Assembly in 1988. Subsequently issued as United Nations sales publication No. E.89.IX.1.

Study on the Economic and Social Consequences of the Arms Race and Military Expenditures (A/43/368): update of the 1982 report of the same title; prepared by the Secretary-General with the assistance of consultant experts pursuant to General Assembly resolutions 40/150 and 41/86 I and submitted to the Assembly in 1988. Subsequently issued as United Nations sales publication No. E.89.IX.2.

Chemical and Bacteriological (Biological) Weapons (A/44/561 and Add.1 and 2): report of the Secretary-General prepared with the assistance of a group of experts pursuant to General Assembly resolutions 42/37 C and 43/74 A and submitted to the Assembly in 1989. The report contains *inter alia* further technical guidelines and procedures for the timely and efficient investigation by the Secretary-General of reports concerning the possible use of chemical and bacteriological (biological) or toxin weapons brought to his attention by any Member State.

Scientific and Technological Developments and Their Impact on International Security (A/45/568): report of the Secretary-General prepared with the assistance of consultant experts pursuant to General Assembly resolution 43/77 A and submitted to the Assembly in 1990.

Comprehensive Study on Nuclear Weapons (A/45/373): update of the 1980 study of the same title; carried out by the Secretary-General with the assistance of governmental experts pursuant to General Assembly resolution 43/75 N and submitted to the Assembly in 1990. Subsequently issued as United Nations sales publication No. E.91.IX.12.

Study on the Role of the United Nations in the Field of Verification (A/45/372 and Corr.1): carried out by the Secretary-General with the assistance of governmental experts pursuant to General Assembly resolution 43/81 B and submitted to the Assembly in 1990. Subsequently issued as United Nations sales publication No. E.91.IX.11.

Study on Effective and Verifiable Measures Which Would Facilitate the Establishment of a Nuclear-Weapon-Free Zone in the Middle East (A/45/435): carried out by the Secretary-General with the assistance of consultant experts pursuant to General Assembly resolution 43/65 and submitted to the Assembly in 1990. Subsequently issued as United Nations sales publication No. E.91.IX.14.

South Africa's Nuclear-Tipped Ballistic Missile Capability (A/45/571 and Corr.l): report of the Secretary-General prepared with the assistance of consultant experts pursuant to General Assembly resolution 44/113 B and submitted to the Assembly in 1990.

Study on Ways and Means of Promoting Transparency in International Transfers of Conventional Arms: (A/46/301) report of the Secretary-General carried out with the assistance of governmental experts pursuant to General Assembly resolution 43/75 I and submitted to the Assembly in 1991. Subsequently issued as United Nations sales publication No. E.93.IX.6.

Study on Charting Potential Uses of Resources Allocated to Military Activities for Civilian Endeavours to Protect the Environment (A/46/364): report of the Secretary-General carried out with the assistance of a group of experts pursuant to General Assembly resolution 45/58 N and submitted to the Assembly in 1991. Issued as a United Nations sales publication under the title *Potential Uses of Military-Related Resources for Protection of the Environment.*

Study of Defensive Security Concepts and Policies (A/47/394): report of the Secretary-General carried out with the assistance of governmental experts pursuant to General Assembly resolution 45/58 O and submitted to the Assembly in 1992.

Report on the Register of Conventional Arms (A/47/342 and Corr.1): report of the Secretary-General on the work of a panel of governmental technical experts appointed pursuant to resolution 46/36 L, which established the Register of Conventional Arms (see page 56). The panel reported on technical procedures for the operation of the Register and modalities for early expansion of its scope.

Studies in Progress

Study on Confidence-building Measures in Outer Space: being carried out by the Secretary-General with the assistance of government experts pursuant to General Assembly resolution 45/55 B for submission to the Assembly at its forth-eighth session, in 1993.

Annex III

Multilateral Arms Regulation and Disarmament Agreements*

Treaty	Content	Dates		Depositaries	Number of Parties[a]
		Opened for signature	Entered into force		
Protocol for the Prohibition of the Use in War of Asphyxiating, Poisonous or Other Gases, and of Bacteriological Methods of Warfare (Geneva Protocol)	Forbids the use in war of chemical and biological weapons. Prohibits the use in international armed conflicts of asphyxiating, poisonous or other gases, and of bacteriological (biological) methods of warfare. Does not forbid the development, production, stockpiling or deployment of chemical or biological weapons.	1925	for each signatory as from the date of deposit of its ratification; accessions take effect on the date of the notification by the depositary Government	France	131
The Antarctic Treaty	Provides for the demilitarization of Antarctica.	1959	23 June 1961	USA	40

*The Chemical Weapons Convention will be opened for signature on 13 January 1993.

[a] Data as of 31 July 1992. See also A/47/470 and Corr.1, "Status of multilateral disarmament agreements".

31

Treaty	Content	Dates		Depositaries	Number of Parties
		Opened for signature	Entered into force		
Treaty Banning Nuclear Weapon Tests in the Atmosphere, in Outer Space and under Water (partial test-ban Treaty)	Bans nuclear tests everywhere except underground. Prohibits all nuclear explosions, for military as well as for peaceful purposes, in the atmosphere, in outer space or under water.	1963	10 October 1963	Russia UK USA	119
Treaty on Principles Governing the Activities of States in the Exploration and Use of Outer Space, including the Moon and Other Celestial Bodies (outer space Treaty)	Prohibits placing nuclear or other weapons of mass destruction in Earth orbit and on the planets, or stationing of such weapons in outer space or on celestial bodies. Lays down the principles governing peaceful activities of States for scientific exploration in outer space. Forbids the establishment of military bases, installations and fortifications, or the testing of any kind of weapon and the conduct of military manoeuvres on celestial bodies.	1967	10 October 1967	Russia UK USA	94

Treaty for the Prohibition of Nuclear Weapons in Latin America and the Caribbean (Treaty of Tlatelolco)	1967	for each Government individually	Mexico	33[b]
Prohibits the testing, use, manufacture, production or acquisition by any means, and the receipt, storage, installation, deployment or any form of possession of any nuclear weapons in Latin America and the Caribbean.				
Treaty on the Non-Proliferation of Nuclear Weapons (non-proliferation Treaty)	1968	5 March 1970	Russia UK USA	150
Provides for the prevention of the spread of nuclear weapons to non-nuclear-weapon States; promotes the process of nuclear disarmament; provides international safeguards to prevent the peaceful nuclear activities of States from being diverted to make nuclear weapons and facilitates access to nuclear technology for peaceful purposes.				

[b] Total includes Brazil, Chile and Dominica, which have not waived the requirements set out in article 28, and the five nuclear-weapon States and the Netherlands, which have ratified one or both of Additional Protocols I and II.

Treaty	Content	Dates		Depositaries	Number of Parties
		Opened for signature	Entered into force		
Treaty on the Prohibition of the Emplacement of Nuclear Weapons and Other Weapons of Mass Destruction on the Sea-Bed and the Ocean Floor and in the Subsoil Thereof (sea-bed Treaty)	Bans the placement of nuclear and other weapons of mass destruction and facilities for such weapons on or under the sea-bed anywhere outside a 12-mile limit from the coast line.	1971	18 May 1972	Russia UK USA	87
Convention on the Prohibition of the Development, Production and Stockpiling of Bacteriological (Biological) and Toxin Weapons and on Their Destruction (biological weapons Convention)	Bans and eliminates all forms of biological weapons.	1972	26 March 1975	Russia UK USA	125

Convention on the Prohibition of Military or Any Other Hostile Use of Environmental Modification Techniques (ENMOD Convention)	Bans the manipulation of nature to cause effects harmful to human welfare, for instance, earthquakes, tidal waves and inundation. Prohibits military or any other hostile use of techniques that would have widespread, long-lasting or sever effects through deliberate manipulation of natural processes.	1977	5 October 1978	Secretary-General of the United Nations	55
Agreement Governing the Activities of States on the Moon and Other Celestial Bodies	Bans the use of the Moon and planets for military purposes. Complements the outer space Treaty, setting aside use of the Moon for peaceful purposes only.	1979	11 July 1984	Secretary-General of the United Nations	8
Convention on Prohibitions or Restrictions on the Use of Certain Conventional Weapons Which May Be Deemed to Be Excessively Injurious or to Have Indiscriminate Effects (inhumane weapons Convention)	Restricts the use of mines, booby traps, incendiary weapons and fragmentation weapons.	1981	2 December 1983	Secretary-General of the United Nations	32

Treaty	Content	Dates		Depositaries	Number of Parties
		Opened for signature	Entered into force		
South Pacific Nuclear Free Zone Treaty (Treaty of Rarotonga)	Forbids parties to possess or control any nuclear explosive device inside or outside the zone. Also forbids them to carry out nuclear testing and commits them to refrain from and prevent the dumping of radioactive waste.	1985	11 December 1986	Secretary General of the Forum Secretariat	13[c]
Treaty on Conventional Armed Forces in Europe (CFE Treaty)	Establishes a balance of conventional forces at lower levels in Europe. Originally negotiated between NATO and the Warsaw Pact.	1990	9 November 1992	The Netherlands	24
Treaty on Open Skies	Establishes an aerial inspection regime by allowing unarmed surveillance flights at short notice over each other's territory of North America, Europe, and the Asian part of Russia.	1992		Canada Hungary	

[c] Total includes the two nuclear-weapon States, China and the Russian Federation, which have ratified Protocols 2 and 3.

Register of Conventional Arms*

1. The Register of Conventional Arms ("the Register") shall be established, with effect from 1 January 1992, and maintained at the Headquarters of the United Nations in New York.

2. Concerning international arms transfers:

(a) Member States are requested to provide data for the Register, addressed to the Secretary-General, on the number of items in the following categories of equipment imported into or exported from their territory:

I. *Battle tanks*

A tracked or wheeled self-propelled armoured fighting vehicle with high cross-country mobility and a high level of self-protection, weighing at least 16.5 metric tonnes unladen weight, with a high muzzle velocity direct fire main gun of at least 75 millimetres calibre.

II. *Armoured combat vehicles*

A tracked or wheeled self-propelled vehicle, with armoured protection and cross-country capability, either: (a) designed and equipped to transport a squad of four or more infantrymen, or (b) armed with an integral or organic weapon of at least 20 millimetres calibre or an anti-tank missile launcher.

III. *Large calibre artillery systems*

A gun, howitzer, artillery piece combining the characteristics of a gun and a howitzer, mortar or multiple-launch rocket system, capable of engaging surface targets by delivering primarily indirect fire, with a calibre of 100 millimetres and above.

* from General Assembly resolution 46/36L

IV. Combat aircraft

A fixed-wing or variable-geometry wing aircraft armed and equipped to engage targets by employing guided missiles, unguided rockets, bombs, guns, cannons, or other weapons of destruction.

V. Attack helicopters

A rotary-wing aircraft equipped to employ anti-armour, air-to-ground, or air-to-air guided weapons and equipped with an integrated fire control and aiming system for these weapons.

VI. Warships

A vessel or submarine with a standard displacement of 850 metric tonnes or above, armed or equipped for military use.

VII. Missiles or missile systems

A guided rocket, ballistic or cruise missile capable of delivering a payload to a range of at least 25 kilometres, or a vehicle, apparatus or device designed or modified for launching such munitions.

(b) Data on imports provided under the present paragraph shall also specify the supplying State; data on exports shall also specify the recipient State and the State of origin if not the exporting State;

(c) Each Member State is requested to provide data on an annual basis by 30 April each year in respect of imports into and exports from their territory in the previous calendar year;

(d) The first such registration shall take place by 30 April 1993 in respect of the calendar year 1992;

(e) The data so provided shall be recorded in respect of each Member State;

(f) Arms "exports and imports" represent in the present resolution, including its annex, all forms of arms transfers under terms of grant, credit, barter or cash.

3. Concerning other interrelated information:

(*a*) Member States are invited also to provide to the Secretary-General available background information regarding their military holdings, procurement through national production, and relevant policies;

(*b*) The information so provided shall be recorded in respect of each Member State.

4. The Register shall be open for consultation by representatives of Member States at any time.

5. In addition, the Secretary-General shall provide annually a consolidated report to the General Assembly of the data registered, together with an index of the other interrelated information.

Dynamics of Arms Expenditures and Military Supplies

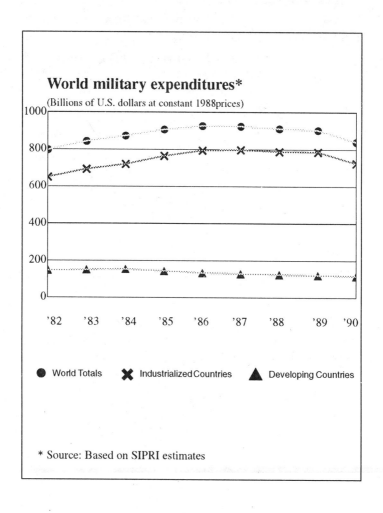

World military expenditures*
(Billions of U.S. dollars at constant 1988prices)

● World Totals ✖ Industrialized Countries ▲ Developing Countries

* Source: Based on SIPRI estimates

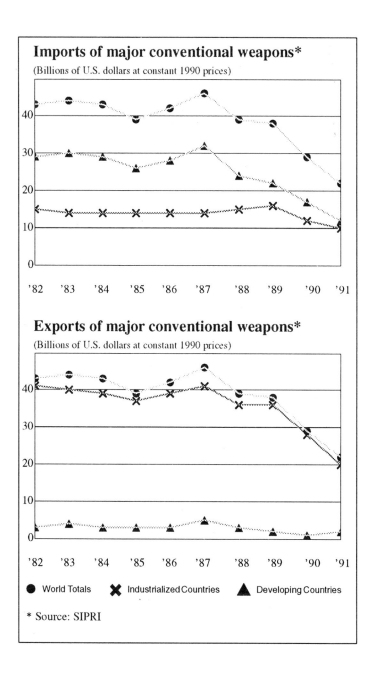

Imports of major conventional weapons*
(Billions of U.S. dollars at constant 1990 prices)

'82 '83 '84 '85 '86 '87 '88 '89 '90 '91

Exports of major conventional weapons*
(Billions of U.S. dollars at constant 1990 prices)

'82 '83 '84 '85 '86 '87 '88 '89 '90 '91

● World Totals   ✖ Industrialized Countries   ▲ Developing Countries

* Source: SIPRI

41

Annex VI
World Military Expenditures*
(As a percentage of gross domestic product)

	1981	1982	1983	1984	1985	1986	1987	1988	1989	1990
North America										
Canada	1.8	2.0	2.1	2.1	2.1	2.1	2.1	2.1	2.0	2.0
USA	5.7	6.3	6.5	6.4	6.6	6.7	6.4	6.1	5.9	5.6
Europe										
Austria	1.2	1.2	1.3	1.2	1.2	1.3	1.2	1.1	1.1	1.0
Belgium	3.4	3.3	3.2	3.1	3.0	3.0	2.9	2.7	2.5	2.4
Bulgaria	3.0	3.3	3.1	3.3	3.4	4.0	4.2	4.4	4.0	3.5
Czechoslovakia	3.1	3.1	3.2	3.3	3.3	3.4	3.4	3.4	3.7	3.1
Denmark	2.5	2.5	2.5	2.3	2.2	2.0	2.1	2.2	2.1	2.0
Finland	1.9	2.1	2.1	2.0	1.9	2.0	1.9	1.9	1.9	1.8
France	4.1	4.1	4.1	4.0	4.0	3.9	4.0	3.8	3.7	3.6
FRGermany	3.4	3.4	3.4	3.3	3.2	3.1	3.1	2.9	2.8	2.8
Germany DR	4.4	4.5	4.5	4.7	4.6	4.8	5.0	5.0	5.0	...
Greece	7.0	6.8	6.3	7.1	7.0	6.2	6.3	6.4	5.7	5.9
Hungary	2.4	2.4	2.4	2.3	3.6	3.6	3.4	3.5	2.8	2.1
Ireland	1.8	1.7	1.5	1.5	1.5	1.6	1.4	1.4	1.3	1.3
Italy	2.1	2.1	2.1	2.2	2.2	2.1	2.3	2.3	2.3	2.1
Luxembourg	1.1	1.0	1.1	1.0	0.9	0.9	1.1	1.1	1.1	1.1
Netherlands	3.2	3.2	3.2	3.2	3.1	3.1	3.1	3.0	2.9	2.7
Norway	2.9	3.0	3.1	2.8	3.1	3.1	3.3	3.2	3.3	3.2
Poland	3.1	3.2	2.8	2.9	3.0	3.6	3.4	3.0	2.0	2.9
Portugal	3.5	3.5	3.3	3.3	3.1	3.2	3.1	3.2	3.2	3.1
Romania	1.6	1.5	1.5	1.4	1.4	1.3	1.2	1.2	1.5	1.4
Spain	2.4	2.4	2.4	2.4	2.4	2.2	2.4	2.1	2.0	1.8
Switzerland	1.8	1.9	1.9	1.9	2.0	1.8	1.7	1.7	1.6	1.6
Sweden	3.0	2.9	2.8	2.7	2.6	2.6	2.5	2.4	2.4	2.4
Turkey	4.9	5.2	4.8	4.4	4.5	4.8	4.2	3.8	4.3	4.9
UK	4.7	5.1	5.1	5.3	5.1	4.9	4.6	4.3	4.1	3.9
USSR	...	...	...	...	...	...	...	...	11.0	...
Yugoslavia	4.5	4.0	3.8	3.7	3.9	4.3	3.9	3.4	2.2	...

*Source: SIPRI estimates.

	1981	1982	1983	1984	1985	1986	1987	1988	1989	1990
Middle East										
Bahrain	5.9	7.5	4.3	3.8	4.2	5.1	5.3	5.0	5.0	...
Cyprus	2.0	1.7	1.7	1.5	1.2	0.9	0.9	1.0	1.2	1.2
Egypt	6.5	6.3	6.7	6.9	5.8	6.1	6.2	4.8	5.2	4.6
Iran	4.3	3.4	2.6	2.5	3.0	3.0	...	...	...	...
Iraq	12.3	18.4	24.3	29.1	26.0	24.2	24.3	23.0	20.0	20.0
Israel	23.5	19.0	20.2	21.4	14.4	11.3	10.2	9.1	8.7	8.4
Jordan	13.7	13.5	13.8	13.1	13.6	14.8	15.0	15.0	10.0	10.9
Kuwait	4.4	6.0	6.8	6.8	7.9	8.6	7.0	7.3	6.5	...
Lebanon	2.4	4.3	12.0	...	...	...	...	...	...	...
Oman	21.0	22.2	24.5	23.9	21.6	23.8	17.6	17.8	15.8	...
Saudi Arabia	14.5	21.1	20.3	20.9	22.0	22.4	22.7	19.8	17.7	...
Syria	14.7	15.6	15.4	16.7	15.6	14.4	11.3	9.2	12.4	13.0
United Arab Emirates	6.3	6.5	6.8	7.0	7.6	8.7	6.7	6.7	5.3	4.7
Yemen Arab Republic	12.6	14.7	14.2	10.4	8.4	7.3	7.2	7.0	...	...
Yemen PDR	19.7	18.7	19.1	17.7	16.7	22.2	18.4	18.5	...	...
South Asia/East Asia										
Bangladesh	1.3	1.5	1.6	1.4	1.3	1.5	1.6	1.6	1.6	...
Brunei	4.5	5.3	6.5	6.5	7.7	...	...	...	...	...
China	...	4.1	3.7	3.2	2.7	2.4	2.3	1.9	2.0	...
Hong Kong	0.9	0.8	0.7	0.6	0.6	0.5	0.5	0.4	...	...
India	3.0	3.1	3.1	3.2	3.3	3.7	3.9	3.5	3.4	3.3
Indonesia	3.7	4.2	3.7	3.5	3.0	3.0	2.5	2.3	2.1	1.6
Japan	0.9	0.9	1.0	1.0	1.0	1.0	1.0	1.0	1.0	1.0
Korea, North	11.5	11.8	12.3	12.0	...	...	9.5	8.7	...	...
Korea, South	6.0	5.8	5.3	4.9	4.9	4.7	4.5	4.6	4.4	4.0
Malaysia	8.1	7.8	5.6	3.8	3.5	5.7	4.5	4.1	4.0	3.6
Mongolia	...	...	...	...	11.2	11.0	11.3	11.7	10.0	10.0
Myanmar	4.1	3.6	3.3	3.3	3.6	3.2	3.0	3.1	3.6	3.5
Nepal	0.9	1.1	1.2	1.2	1.3	1.6	1.8	1.8	1.7	...
Pakistan	5.9	6.6	6.9	6.8	6.8	7.1	7.1	6.7	6.7	6.6
Philippines	2.2	2.3	2.2	1.5	1.3	1.4	1.3	1.3	1.8	1.8
Singapore	5.1	5.1	4.5	5.5	6.5	6.3	5.8	5.5	5.1	5.0

43

	1981	1982	1983	1984	1985	1986	1987	1988	1989	1990
Sri Lanka	1.2	1.1	1.4	1.4	3.2	4.4	5.1	4.3	3.3	4.8
Taiwan	6.7	7.3	6.8	6.1	6.4	5.9	6.3	6.0	6.0	6.0
Thailand	4.8	4.9	5.0	5.0	5.0	4.7	4.3	4.0	3.2	3.2
Africa										
Algeria	1.8	1.9	1.9	1.8	1.7	1.7	1.7	1.5	1.5	...
Angola	13.8	11.9	16.5	22.0	28.4	28.4	...	21.5	20.0	...
Benin	1.8	1.9	2.2	2.0	2.0	1.9	2.0	2.0	...	...
Botswana	3.7	2.7	2.4	2.4	2.1	2.7	4.1	2.7	2.5	...
Burkina Faso	2.8	3.0	2.9	3.0	2.5	3.5	3.0	2.8	...	...
Burundi	3.0	3.5	3.1	3.2	3.0	3.4	2.7	2.2	...	...
Cameroon	1.1	1.7	2.2	2.1	2.2	2.1	2.1	2.1	...	...
Central African Republic	2.1	2.0	2.6	2.3	2.0	1.8	1.7	1.8	...	...
Chad	...	7.0	7.8	5.7	6.0	4.0	...	...	...	...
Congo	2.1	2.3	2.3	2.3	2.6	4.0	...	3.2	...	...
Côte d'Ivoire	1.1	1.1	1.1	1.1	1.0	1.0	1.2	1.2	...	...
Ethiopia	8.4	8.4	8.4	9.0	8.9	8.9	10.0	12.2	13.5	...
Gabon	2.4	2.4	2.6	2.3	2.6	4.0	4.3	4.5	...	...
Ghana	0.7	0.7	0.5	0.6	1.0	0.9	0.9	0.5	0.6	0.6
Kenya	3.6	3.8	3.6	2.9	2.4	2.9	3.0	2.6	2.5	2.4
Liberia	4.8	4.3	2.3	2.4	2.3	2.2	...	...	...	...
Libya	14.0	15.0	13.0	14.5	15.2	12.7	10.0	8.6	...	...
Madagascar	3.0	2.7	2.4	2.3	2.2	2.2	1.8	1.4	...	...
Malawi	3.3	2.4	1.9	1.6	1.5	1.8	1.6	1.7	1.6	1.5
Mali	2.4	2.4	2.4	2.7	2.3	...	...	3.2	...	...
Mauritania	7.6	6.9	5.7	...	...	...	...	...	...	...
Mauritius	0.4	0.3	0.3	0.2	0.2	0.2	0.2	0.2	0.3	0.2
Morocco	6.6	6.5	4.9	4.7	5.4	5.1	5.0	4.2	4.4	4.5
Mozambique	8.0	10.7	12.1	11.7	10.4	...	...	...	...	...
Niger	0.7	0.6	0.7	0.7	0.7	0.8	0.8	0.8	0.8	...
Nigeria	2.3	1.8	1.9	1.3	1.2	1.2	0.7	0.9	0.9	0.9
Rwanda	2.0	2.0	1.9	1.6	1.6	1.9	1.8	1.7	1.7	1.7
Senegal	2.8	2.8	2.7	2.7	2.5	2.2	2.0	2.0	...	...
Sierra Leone	1.0	0.8	0.7	0.7	0.6	1.1	0.8	0.5	0.6	0.7
Somalia	4.3	3.4	3.8	2.7	1.8	1.8	1.8	3.0	...	...

South Africa	4.0	4.1	4.0	4.0	4.1	4.2	4.5	4.6	4.7	4.3
Sudan	2.0	1.7	2.1	3.9	2.6	2.1	2.0	2.0	...	...
Swaziland	2.2	2.9	2.6	2.3	1.8	1.7	...	...	...	...
Tanzania	4.3	4.2	3.9	3.8	3.8	4.7	4.7	5.2	6.9	...
Togo	2.4	2.3	2.2	2.3	2.6	2.5	2.6	3.2	...	...
Tunisia	2.7	5.9	6.6	4.7	5.2	5.9	5.5	5.3	4.8	3.2
Uganda	3.8	2.7	3.0	5.0	5.9	3.8	3.5	1.7	0.8	...
Zaire	1.3	1.0	1.4	1.5	3.5	2.0	3.1	2.0	3.9	1.2
Zambia	4.4	4.1	3.9	3.0	2.4	3.7	3.2	3.2	...	...
Zimbabwe	6.4	5.7	5.7	6.2	5.7	6.2	6.5	7.3	...	...
Latin America										
Argentina	7.1	6.0	4.6	4.5	3.5	3.7	3.3	3.5	3.3	...
Bolivia	5.3	4.5	3.9	3.4	3.4	2.8	2.9	3.1	3.3	3.2
Brazil	1.3	1.6	1.2	1.2	1.1	1.2	1.1	1.4	1.5	1.7
Chile	7.4	9.5	8.0	9.6	7.6	8.0	6.8	7.8	6.6	5.0
Colombia	1.8	1.8	2.3	2.4	2.1	2.0	2.0	2.3	2.6	2.7
Costa Rica	0.6	0.5	0.7	0.7	0.6	0.6	0.5	0.4	0.5	0.5
Cuba	8.8	9.1	8.8	10.1	9.6	10.2	10.7	11.3	10.0	...
Dom. Republic	1.7	1.6	1.5	1.6	1.4	1.3	1.3	1.1	0.8	0.8
El Salvador	3.7	4.4	4.4	4.6	4.4	4.9	3.8	3.7	3.5	2.9
Ecuador	1.7	1.7	1.6	1.5	1.8	1.9	2.0	1.7	1.6	1.5
Guatemala	1.9	1.9	2.0	2.2	2.0	1.6	1.5	1.6	1.4	1.2
Guyana	6.0	5.4	4.8	4.9	8.9	5.6	3.2	2.8	2.5	1.9
Haiti	1.4	1.3	1.2	1.1	1.2	1.4	1.5	1.5	1.6	1.5
Honduras	2.3	2.8	4.0	5.2	6.4	5.9	5.5	5.6	8.4	6.9
Jamaica	1.6	1.7	1.4	1.1	1.1	0.9	0.8	...	...	...
Mexico	0.6	0.5	0.5	0.6	0.7	0.6	0.5	0.5	0.4	...
Nicaragua	5.3	6.0	10.3	10.9	23.2	20.9	34.2	28.3	...	...
Panama	1.2	1.3	1.4	1.9	1.9	2.0	2.0	2.5	2.7	2.5
Paraguay	1.5	1.6	1.4	1.2	1.1	1.1	1.1	1.0	1.3	1.0
Peru	6.0	8.5	8.1	5.6	6.4	6.6	5.0	2.5	2.1	2.1
Trinidad & Tobago	2.3	2.9	2.9	2.6	2.6	2.7	...	...	...	...
Uruguay	3.9	4.0	3.2	2.6	2.4	2.3	2.1	2.1	2.1	2.1
Venezuela	3.1	3.4	2.9	2.4	2.0	2.1	2.1	1.9	2.2	2.0

Oceania

Australia	2.6	2.7	2.8	2.8	2.8	2.8	2.6	2.2	2.3	2.3
Fiji	1.3	1.3	1.3	1.3	1.2	1.2	2.1	2.3	2.5	...
New Zealand	2.1	2.1	2.0	1.9	1.9	2.0	2.0	2.1	2.1	2.0

INDEX

(The numbers following the entries refer to page numbers in the report and in the six annexes)

Combat zones, 8

Comprehensive approaches, 16

Comprehensive study on nuclear weapons, 29

Conference on Disarmament, 15, 22

Confidence−building/ measures, 9, 10, 12, 18
study on CBMs in outer space, 30
See also regional agreements/disarmament

Conflict resolution, 7, 8

Conventional arms/capabilities/disarmament, 4, 10, 12, 17
report on the register on conventional arms, 30
See also transparency in armaments

Conversion. *See* economic aspects of disarmament

D

Defensive security concepts, study on, 30

Deployment of weapons of mass destruction, 13

Destruction and storage of armaments, 20, 21

Disarmament by mutual example, 9

Disengagement zones, 7

Dismantling weapons, 20

Disposal/destruction of arms, 8, 21

Dual−use technologies, 16
See also science and technology

E

Early warning instruments, 19

Economic aspects of disarmament
conversion, 20
study on economic and social consequences of the arms race and military expenditures, 28

ENMOD Convention, 35

Environment, 21
study on resources for military use and civilian endeavours to protect the environment, 30

Excessive accumulations of armaments, 18

Expenditures on arms. *See* military expenditures

Expert report on South Africa, 29

Export controls. *See* arms transfers

Exports and imports of arms/equipment, 37, 41

F

Final Document of the Tenth special Session of the General Assembly, 27

G

General Assembly, special sessions. *See* Special Sessions

Geneva Protocol (1925), 31

Global arms reduction, 10

Global multilateral agreements, 12

Globalization of disarmament, 4, 5, 9, 11

I

ICBM. *See* intercontinental ballistic missiles

Inhumane Weapons Convention, 35

Inspection. *See* weapons inspection

Integration, 4, 5

Intercontinental ballistic missiles, 13

International behaviour, 6

International peace and security, 4, 7

International security system, 9

L

Land—mines, 8

Large calibre artillery systems, 38

Legitimate defensive needs, 17

Long—range delivery systems, 16

Long—range nuclear warheads, 13

M

Military expenditures, 3, 6, 7, 17, 40, 42–46
reduction, 12

Military holdings, 39

Military Staff Committee, 22

Missiles or missile systems, 38

Monitoring troop withdrawals, 7

Moratoria on nuclear testing, 15

Multilateral arms regulation and disarmament agreements, 31

Multilateral arrangements, 9

N

National security, 9

Non–proliferation, 6, 15, 16, 18
See also arms transfers; non–proliferation Treaty

Non–proliferation Treaty, 4, 16
extension in 1995, 16

Non–threatening intentions, 19

Nuclear disarmament, 9, 10, 13, 33

Nuclear testing, 14
moratoria, 15
nuclear–test ban, 15

Nuclear weapons
number of nuclear weapons test, 14–15
study on a nuclear–weapon–free zone in the Middle East, 29
study on nuclear weapons, 29

Nuclear–weapon–free/nuclear–free zones, 29
See also Treaty of Rarotonga; Treaty of Tlatelolco

O

Objective information. See transparency

Open Skies Treaty, 36

Opportunities costs, 17

Outer space, 13
Agreement on celestial bodies, 35
outer space Treaty, 32
study on confidence–building measures in outer space, 30

P

Partial test–ban treaty, 32

Peace enforcement, 8

Peace–building, 7

Peace–keeping, 7

Peacemaking, 7

Political process, 6

Post–disarmament issues, 20

Preventive diplomacy, 7, 19

Production overcapacities, 16

Proliferation, 6, 12, 13
See also non−proliferation

Q

Qualitative improvement of nuclear weapons, 14

R

Reciprocated unilateral measures. *See* disarmament by mutual example

Regional agreements/disarmament, 10, 12, 17
See also confidence−building/measure; conventional disarmament

Regional organizations, 10

Regional security and stability, 10

Register of conventional arms, 18, 37
report on the register of conventional arms, 30

Revitalization, 4, 5

Risk of conflict, 10

S

Safeguards, 16
See also IAEA

Science and technology, 16
study on scientific and technological developments, 28
See also arms transfers; dual−use technologies

Seabed Treaty, 13, 34

Security Council
implementation of resolution 687 (1991), 8
involvement in disarmament matters, 22
Summit of January 1991, 15

South Africa, study on South Africa's nuclear−tipped ballistic missile capability, 29

South Pacific. *See* Treaty of Rarotonga

Special Sessions of the General Assembly Devoted to Disarmament, 27

Standardized reporting. *See* arms transfers, military budgets/expenditures

START, 13

Studies
on a nuclear−weapon−free zone in the Middle East, 29

W

Warships, 38

Weapons control, 7

Weapons disposal. *See* disposal/destruction of arms

Weapons inspection, 7, 8

Weapons of mass destruction, 6, 12, 15, 16
See also specific items in index

Weapons proliferation, 6

Litho. in United Nations, New York
92-84318—January 1993—3,200
ISBN 92-1-142192-6

United Nations publication
Sales No. E.93.IX.8